THE NEW YORK DOG

RACHAEL HALE McKENNA

THE NEW YORK DOG

RACHAEL HALE McKENNA

Stewart, Tabori & Chang, New York
in association with PQ Blackwell

FOREWORD

GEORGINA BLOOMBERG

We New Yorkers are a tough group. We put up with being called rude, egotistical, pushy, arrogant, and loud. You name it, we've heard it; some of us even find pride in being called so. Like an initiation or a stamp of authenticity, these labels mean to some that they are true New Yorkers.

We take pride in breaking the rules and not being like everyone else—jaywalking, not obeying traffic regulations, and testing the limits of every other law and rule placed on us are things that seem normal. We stand just a few feet off the street curb to show we aren't afraid and that we won't be held back by something like oncoming cars. It's like we are standing our ground and making a statement just with those few steps. We glance around at the poor law-abiding citizens who are hanging back safely on the sidewalk, as if taking pity on their lack of ambition, and then we will take off to cross the street whenever *we* deem acceptable, regardless of the signal. The thrill of pushing limits and breaking the rules is in our blood. We are ambitious, tough, and confident. We don't waste time by walking or talking slowly, and while others may think we come off as unfriendly, we just see it as concentrating on getting ahead.

But we New Yorkers have a secret that we don't want the rest of the world knowing. . . . We love our dogs. For a few hours each morning and again each evening, we congregate in our city's parks and grassy areas to do something we would never admit to—we let down our guard. We slow down our pace, and we become selfless, loving, friendly, and courteous to others. We smile at and chat with strangers just because they have dogs, too. We forget about our other responsibilities and ambitions, and we take a few moments away from trying to conquer the world. We even do something unheard of by most New Yorkers: we follow the rules! We diligently pick up our dog's poop and observe the times our dogs can be off the leash. We are even proud of our compliance with the law, giving each other an approving nod of the head when we spot someone with a poop bag.

Go to a park first thing in the morning and you will see these "tough, rude, and self-centered" people with beaming faces, rain or shine, no matter the temperature, as they smile and greet each other, and admire their canine family members. I guarantee you; it's the only time you will see two New Yorkers make eye contact and say hello without knowing each other.

When we step back onto the street we quickly gather ourselves, picking our pace back up. We glance around to make sure no one saw the exhibition of emotion and friendliness we just demonstrated, and we stare straight ahead to avoid looking at one another in the eye. We wipe the smiles off our faces so that people are reminded that we are tough New Yorkers and not to be messed with. We go back to concentrating on our busy schedules, and how we are going to get ahead in the world today. But, there is a little spark in our eyes and a curl at the edges of our lips that we sometimes can't hide as we think about the joy that the time with our cherished canine companions and other dog parents has just brought us. We, of course, try our best to cover this up with the typical New York behavior and attitude that others like to call coldhearted or rude, but there is no denying it.

We know that having dogs in our lives has softened us and keeps us human. We may be scowling on the outside, but it's just an act. On the inside we are glowing and stealing adoring glances at our four-legged best friends whom we love so deeply. This secret is one that we guard closely. Don't tell anyone, OK?

Left: Georgina Bloomberg with her five rescue dogs: Chopper, Hugo, Mabel, Mona, and Stella, and Wilbur, her rescue pig.

ALL THE NEW YORK DOGS

New York, New York! Big city, huge character, and an enormous number of dogs.

To be honest, I didn't know where to start with this book. The more I looked and the more I researched, the bigger the challenge became. Thankfully, that's what I thrive on, and this has been one of my most enjoyable, exciting, and fun-filled projects to date.

I thought that leaving a quiet southern French lifestyle and throwing my family into the loud, chaotic madness of life in the Big Apple would be overwhelming, but we were definitely ready for it. We have all truly fallen in love with our surroundings. Even our daughter, Charlize, is in her element—she loves to talk and has discovered that New Yorkers do, too! But, first and foremost, I don't think I have visited another city where dogs are so loved and treated with so much care. Honestly, New Yorkers adore their dogs.

It's not a place that you would automatically associate with dogs, but I have seen more dogs here than in any other major city I have visited. Not surprising, considering New York has an estimated dog population of 1.5 million. Having spent the previous three years traveling and shooting images of the French countryside, the thought of photographing such an iconic city, full of concrete, cars, and people, was daunting, especially as this is one of the most photographed cities in the world. I wanted to capture something new and fresh, but, more important, I wanted to illustrate the true essence of

life in New York for its canine inhabitants, be they pampered apartment dogs, Central Park dogs, dogs that accompany their owners to the deli and to the cinema, or dogs that are treasured family members.

In some ways *The New York Dog* has been a more complex project than *The French Dog*. In France I was usually able to photograph any dog anywhere. They freely wander the streets in rural villages, and often the dog's owner wouldn't even be around for me to ask their permission. But this wasn't the case in New York City, where dog laws require all dogs in public spaces to be on leashes unless they're in a designated off-leash area. I had to strike up conversations with the owners and organize to meet up another day before capturing the images. I developed relationships with these dog-loving New Yorkers, and many people told me stories about their cherished pets— Oscar the rescued dog (page 119), motorbike-riding Pork Chop (page 39), and adored companions Valentino and Geisha (page 105). I was also lucky enough to spend time with the Humane Society of New York. The work they do in caring for abandoned and uncared-for animals is so humbling. It was wonderful to witness the care and attention given to these dogs so they can have a second chance.

I'd heard of the New York Police Department's unique K-9 unit, which has over one hundred detection and patrol dogs.

Central Park is a dog's dream and every day, before nine in the morning and after nine at night, dogs are allowed to dash about to their hearts' content.

Hoping to meet one of these amazing dogs, I contacted the department and they arranged a meeting with police officer Scott Mateyaschuk and his dog, Aragon. Together they have rescued victims from earthquake and hurricane disaster zones. I photographed them at the department's training facility in Brooklyn. Though I was hiding beneath the rubble in one of the facility's simulated disaster zones, it only took seconds for Aragon to find me.

We had the opportunity to photograph some well-known New Yorkers and their dogs, including actress and dog-lover Tracy Middendorf. It was a thrill to meet photographer William Wegman, whose Weimaraners are famous for their appearances on *Sesame Street*, and fashion photographer Albert Watson and his dog, Miki. I felt total admiration for the incredible work Broadway animal trainer Bill Berloni does supporting the Humane Society of New York.

Growing up with dogs in the green, open spaces of New Zealand, I was curious to learn about the life of a dog in the city of New York. While they don't have twenty-four-hour access to outdoor areas in which they can run freely, they do have some spectacular parks. Central Park is a dog's dream and every day, before nine in the morning and after nine at night, dogs are allowed to dash about to their hearts' content. Owners congregate in groups according to the size of their dogs, regular dog attendees running loops of excitement around each other on first greeting, and the owners' main topic of conversation? Dogs, of course!

For New Yorkers, not only does owning a dog provide wonderful companionship, but also it's an escape from the daily

Dog walkers out exercising New Yorkers' beloved pups are a common sight—a gang of hounds eagerly pulling on their leads, loving the smells and noises of the street.

grind of work in the concrete jungle, offering a chance to get away from the office and venture into the green world of one of the parks. You can see their stress dissipate as they watch their four-legged friends frolic with fellow dogs and as they walk among the trees in the city's oases. I fell in love with Prospect Park in Brooklyn. It is not quite as big as Central Park, but it is wilder and feels more isolated. Within the park you'll come across the Peninsula—I almost don't want to mention it, it is such a paradise, and not just for dogs. Walking around the edge of the lake feels like being in the middle of the countryside. During the week you will see only two or three people there, throwing sticks for their dogs.

New York City dogs are incredibly social; during the five months we were there, I never once witnessed a dogfight. The dogs are loved, well looked after, and treated with total respect. Many owners walk their dog before and after work, and often they will also employ a dog walker to take their dog out during the day. Dog walkers out exercising New Yorkers' beloved pups are a common sight—a gang of hounds eagerly pulling on their leads, loving the smells and noises of the street. Or if at all possible, dog owners will head home at lunchtime for another cuddle with their favorite pooch and sometimes to take them out for a breath of fresh air.

My experience creating *The New York Dog* has been life-changing. As a family we have fully embraced life in New York, so much so that we would love to return to live and work here. We're looking forward to our traveling being over and to settling down to more adventures in New York City, with our own dog in tow.

Rachael Hale McKenna

People in New York . . . love dogs, as if they're grateful for animal presence in the angled and concrete realm in which they dwell.

MARK DOTY (Poet)

RILEY

I was very excited to meet Riley—he sounded like such a gorgeous character, and I had never met any of these popular beagle crossbreeds. Riley is a beabull, a mix between an English bulldog and a beagle, and he is adorable; such a placid, friendly, loveable rogue. I spent the morning with Riley and his owner, capturing some images of him at home, and then wandering the gorgeous quaint streets of Greenwich Village and across to the Hudson River, which lines the west side of Manhattan. Riley was the perfect model, sitting and striking a pose whenever and wherever I requested.

Impeccably groomed and ready to impress, the dogs of New York share the same style and flair as their hometown.

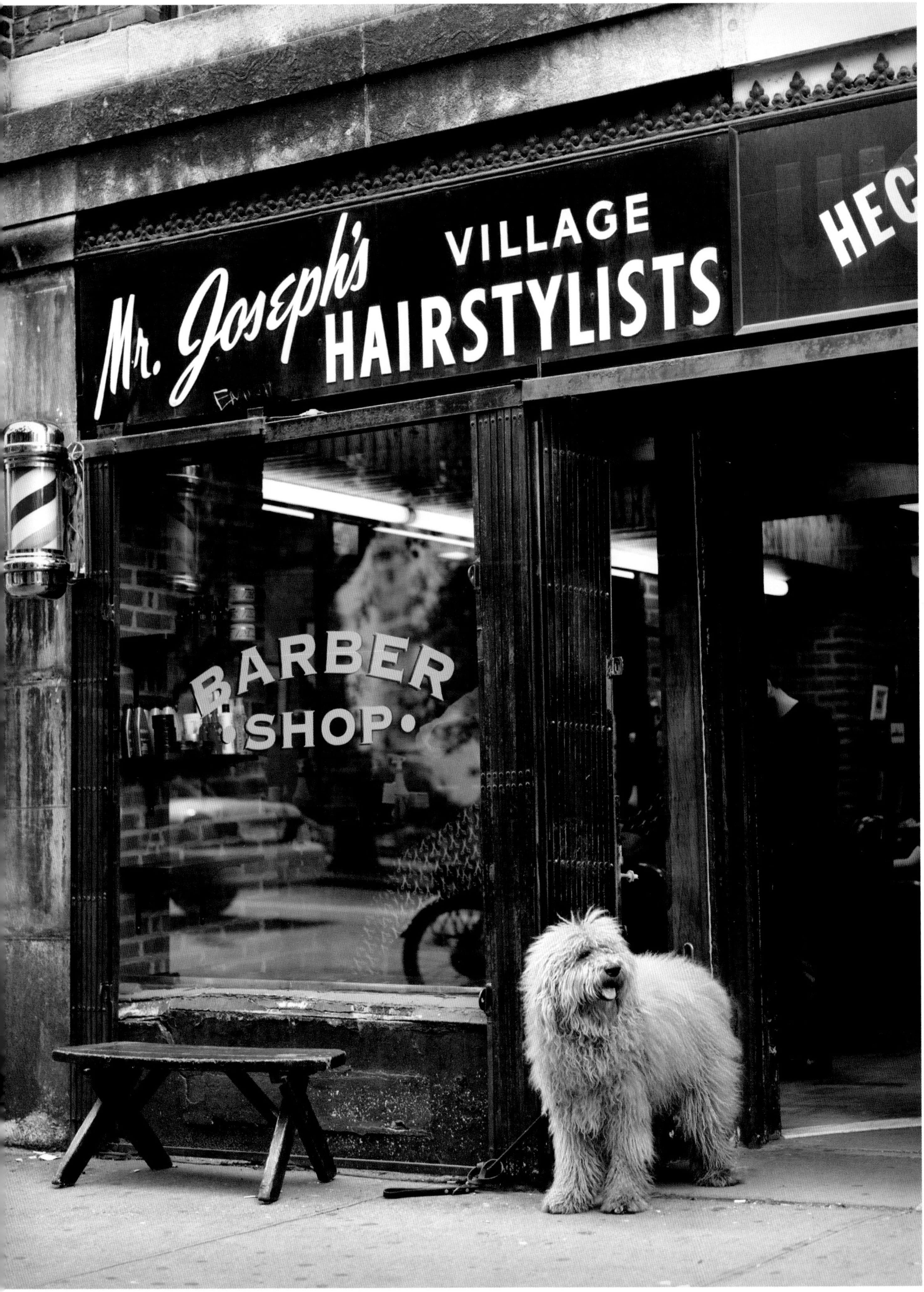
Mr. Joseph's
VILLAGE
HAIRSTYLISTS
BARBER
SHOP

After living in New York for ten years and never really knowing my neighbors, I now know all my neighbors because everyone has a dog. You get to know people through their dogs.

ALISON PACE (Writer)

ANDY WARHOL (Artist)

Famous New Yorker and prince of the pop art movement, Andy Warhol was known to be a cat lover. However, in the 1970s he acquired a miniature dachshund whom he named Archie. The small dog became Warhol's constant companion, accompanying him to his studio, art openings, and gala events. Archie often dined out with Warhol at Ballato's restaurant in SoHo, where he would sit on Warhol's lap, disguised by a napkin in case the health inspector visited. He even became Warhol's alter ego during interviews. When asked a question that he was reluctant to answer, Warhol would deflect to Archie. Later, Warhol adopted a second dachshund, Amos, and the two dogs would chase each other around Warhol's apartment. Following their iconic owner's death, the two dogs were cared for by one of Warhol's friends, living until they were nineteen and twenty years old.

PORK CHOP

I met Pork Chop, a gorgeous little French bulldog/Boston terrier mix, and his owners, Cameron and Shelby, on one of my trips to the Brooklyn neighborhood of DUMBO (Down Under the Manhattan Bridge Overpass). When Shelby told me that their dog often rode with them on their motorbike, I knew this was something I wanted to capture. So early one morning, we proceeded to entertain the local work-goers with Cam riding up and down the quiet streets, Pork Chop displaying incredible balance just sitting on the back of the motorbike. Though this looked great for the photo, it wasn't the safest mode of transport to portray for a dog, so we captured an image of the normal way Pork Chop traveled by bike: in a backpack worn on Cam's chest. Although, in order for him to be more visible for the photo, we did have him popping a little farther out of the bag than normal!

I've seen a look in dogs' eyes, a quickly vanishing look of amazed contempt, and I am convinced that basically dogs think humans are nuts.

JOHN STEINBECK (Writer)

Dogs are an ever-present part of the heart and soul of the city. NYC pooches are street-smart and social. They readily accept humans as part of their pack.

MIKI

"Miki arrived just three days before Christmas. From the first moment it wasn't about whether or not we were going to keep her but whether or not she decided to stay. Thank God she's still here! Miki is a wonderful combination of fire and cool, pure energy all day long and calm in the evening when she lies curled up in my lap in front of the fire. Wonderfully naughty at times, she obviously didn't like my book on Las Vegas as she ate half of it! But I always forgive her—three licks on my nose and she can do anything. Over the years I've received many fabulous Christmas presents, but none compare with Miki."

Albert Watson (Photographer)

LILY AND REYKJAVIK

After finishing a shoot with another dog one morning, I was strolling along the East River and saw these two magnificent dogs being walked by their owners. I just couldn't pass by this opportunity; I approached them and asked if they would mind if I photographed the great Danes with the Manhattan Bridge in the background. They were thrilled, especially one of the owners who was about to move with her Dane to Hawaii—it would be a wonderful memory of the two best friends, commonly known in the neighborhood as "The DUMBO Danes."

P. G. WODEHOUSE (Writer)

English humorist P. G. Wodehouse had a huge affection for dogs and they frequently appear in his short stories and novels. He and his wife, Ethel, were living in France when the Second World War broke out. Unlike many other foreigners living abroad, they delayed their return to the United Kingdom because they couldn't bear the thought of leaving their beloved dogs behind. Consequently, when Germany invaded France, Wodehouse was interned in Germany for almost a year. He and Ethel immigrated to the United States in the 1950s and settled in Remsenburg, Long Island, where they owned a large number of dogs, including a succession of Pekingese named Bimmy, Boo, Loopy, Mrs. Miffen, Squeaky, Miss Winks, and Wonder. In 1966, the Wodehouses generously donated $20,000 to the Bide-A-Wee Association so that it could build the P. G. Wodehouse Shelter for stray animals in Westhampton.

Let Rover rove!

SLOGAN OF THE URBAN CANINE CONSERVANCY

GRAVY

During July we experienced our first New York City heat wave. I thought the South of France was hot, but it is nothing compared to the heat that bounces off the concrete and brick surroundings of New York. With no breeze, the heat is exhausting. The only escape is to stay inside where there is air-conditioning or to go swimming. I felt the most sorry for the dogs—even in the early hours of the morning there was no avoiding the heat. It made photographing them almost impossible, unless I wanted images of dogs with their tongues hitting the sidewalk, and the sidewalk was too hot even for their feet! Charlize was always eager to help out during the early morning shoots, and Gravy was just as eager to be watered.

ROXY

I was sitting in a bar in Brooklyn one evening when, to my great excitement, I saw a man walking along the other side of the street with a dog that was the spitting image of my old dog Kizzie! I took chase. Like Kizzie did, Roxy walks fast, so by the time I caught up to them, I was dripping from sprinting in the summer heat—not the best look when you are trying to be professional, but I didn't want to lose this dog. When we later got together to create the images, I was overwhelmed at the similarities Roxy shared with Kizzie. It made me miss my girl, and highlighted my yearning to own another dog. Thankfully, in the meantime I get to work with dogs every day.

You Gotta Have Bark in Prospect Park.

SLOGAN

PLUTO

"We adopted Pluto from a shelter in Los Angeles when he was just two months old. He has been our friend, our protector, and our joy. We now live in Brooklyn and he reminds us every day how to enjoy this town. The highlights of his day are walking off-leash through Fort Greene Park every morning and cruising the neighborhood of brownstones every evening. He's helped us make friends while befriending other dogs and forces us to stop and take in the beauty of the seasons. My boys have grown up with him, and we can't imagine our family without him. My husband likes to say that he's a mix between a dachshund and a terrier, so that makes him either a toxin or a derrière. Pluto doesn't seem to mind being the 'butt' of a joke."

Tracy Middendorf (Actor)

If your dog is fat, you aren't getting enough exercise.

ANONYMOUS

FLO, TOPPER, CANDY, AND BOBBIN

"One of the great things about having a dog—or in my case, four dogs—in the city is that it encourages you to socialize. You can meet interesting people for about five minutes, which is a nice chunk of time. Some people know the dogs from *Sesame Street*, others from calendars and children's books, but most people just know the dogs as dogs, which is what they really are."

William Wegman (Artist)

Volume 1: Best of the first Decade 1969-1979

THE CRYSTAL BALL OF POP

SANDRA J. BRANT

Andy Warhol Interview

Fifth Avenue is too expensive for anyone but dogs.

MEL FINKELSTEIN (Photographer)

THE NEW YORK PALACE

Comprising the historic monument Villard Mansion along with a fifty-five-story tower, the New York Palace is one of Manhattan's premier luxury hotels. But not only does it offer sumptuous accommodation and refined dining, it is also pet friendly—dogs weighing under twenty-five pounds are welcome in its rooms, suites, and apartments.

VALENTINO AND GEISHA

"We adopted Valentino from an animal shelter. He is fifty percent German shepherd, thirty percent Norwegian elkhound, and twenty percent Afghan (we had his DNA tested). The shelter named him Valentino because he was found around Valentine's Day. When we're out walking, Valentino likes to stop and high-five people. Most people who meet him think that he is a little human in a dog's body.

Three years after we adopted Valentino, we decided to adopt another dog, a Pekingese we named Geisha. She travels everywhere with me and is extremely calm. I call her my shadow. In the beginning, Valentino was not very happy about having another dog in the house, and he completely ignored Geisha for a good year and a half. Now he is very protective of her. If she is having a bath, he puts his paws on the bathtub and cries to be put in the bath with her. It might sound crazy, but I often think that they work together to get their own way. If we have to travel, a friend stays at our house with them. If he can't, we have another friend that travels from France to be with them. Perhaps we are crazy, but they have given me a new outlook on life."

Ginetta Bernard (Dog owner, Washington Heights, Manhattan)

SANDY

"In 1976, when I was nineteen years old, I met a dog that would change my life. I was an apprentice at the Goodspeed Opera House in East Haddam, Connecticut. That summer was the world premiere of the musical *Annie*, about Little Orphan Annie and her dog, Sandy. The theater realized they could not afford a dog trainer, so when I was offered a part in one of their plays in exchange for training the dog, I jumped at the chance. I heard that there were cheap dogs at the local animal shelter so off I went, casting for Sandy. On my first day I found a dog who looked like the part. He had been abused and was going to be put to sleep the next day. I adopted him for seven dollars. Less than a year later, *Annie* opened on Broadway. Sandy became a star, and I became a famous animal trainer. Thirty-five years later, after working on dozens of Broadway shows and receiving a Tony Honor for Excellence in Theatre, I find myself back on Broadway with the most recognizable Broadway animal character ever: Sandy, now played by my dear Sunny, who, like the original Sandy, was found in a shelter the day before she was to be euthanized. New York is for dreamers who come here and hope for fame and fortune. For the hundreds of animals I have rescued, not only do they find fame, but we are also able to give them a second chance at life and a permanent home. Only in NYC."

Bill Berloni (Broadway animal trainer)

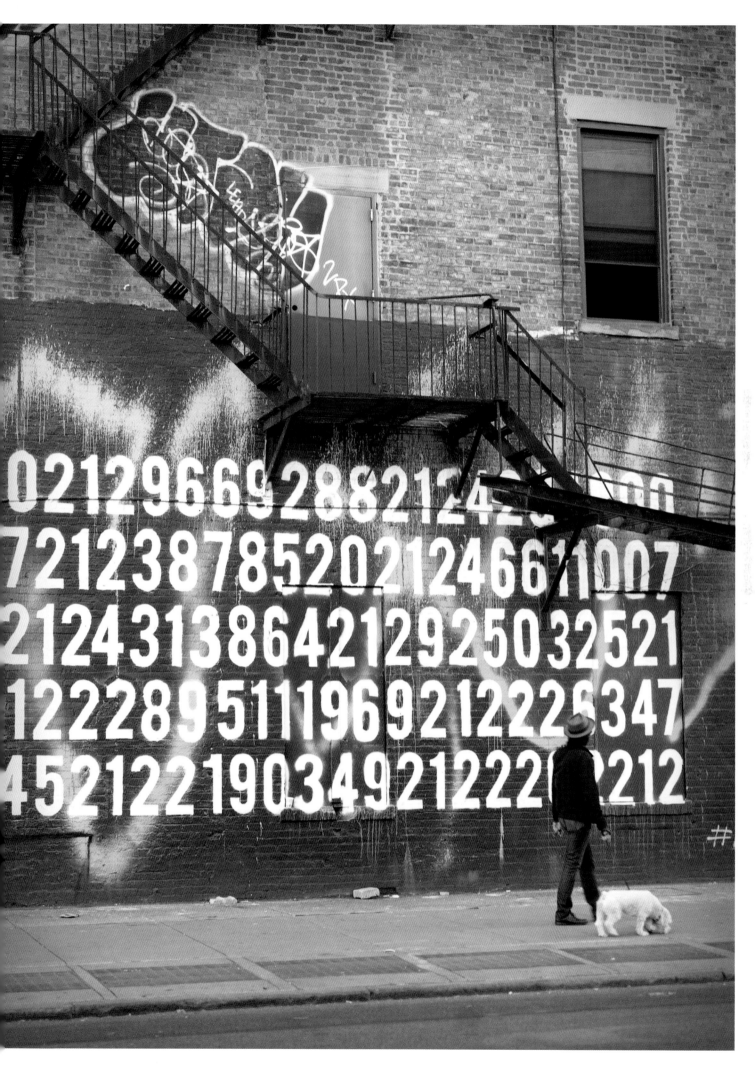

OSCAR

"I discovered Oscar outside my office building in Queens on a cold day. He had been abused and his head was bleeding profusely. He came to me and nuzzled his head in my coat. The vet told me Oscar had a twenty percent chance of survival. It took almost a year before he recovered enough for me to take him home. I knew I wasn't allowed to have a dog, so I tried to find him an owner, but no one wanted a dog with any kind of 'pit' in him. So I made up my mind: I'd keep him and take my chances with the landlord. I was determined to make it work and eventually my landlord fell in love with him—Oscar put on the charm.

When I take him for his walk in the morning, he offers his paw to everyone waiting for the bus. Some drivers let him get on the bus and run from the front to the back. We go to Burger King once a week, and he gets two plain hamburgers and they all know him. He saved me one morning when I was almost mugged. He had the man on the ground before I even knew he was behind me. Oscar is such a sweet dog. But no one will let him play with their dogs in the dog park or on the street. They see the scar on his head and think he is mean and that he has been a fighting dog. He's not mean, he just wants to play, and he gets lonely sometimes. They just judge him on his looks and don't give him a chance. It breaks my heart."

Bobbie Plachko (Dog owner, Queens)

REDMOND AND MONTY

If you want to browse a bookstore and sit on the couch flicking through pages of the latest releases with your dog curled up beside you, then BookCourt in Cobble Hill is the place to go. Henry, BookCourt's owner, loves dogs and always has an open door to customers wanting to enter and browse with their dogs in tow. To convey this idea, Zac, Henry's son, and his Saint Bernard, Redmond, plus Henry's new rescue pup, Monty, all posed for me in the relaxed atmosphere of this wonderful bookstore.

For names, New Yorkers favor Princess, Bella, and Lola for females, and Max, Rocky, and Lucky for males. On Wall Street you're likely to see Coco strutting along, whereas the West Village is home to many Charlies.

Dogs are obsessed with being happy.

JAMES THURBER (Writer, cartoonist, and humorist)

MERLIN

On a fresh, frosty February morning, my husband, Andy, and I were exploring the neighborhood of DUMBO, in Brooklyn, for the first time. Sitting on the edge of the East River, overlooking Manhattan, the buildings in DUMBO are weathered and full of character, a dream location for photography. Merlin, an adorable pit bull mix, was out on his morning walk, so I approached Tom, his owner, and asked if he could spare a few minutes for me to photograph Merlin. The combination of the light, the backdrop, and a very happy dog resulted in a wonderful image portraying the industrial play spaces New York City has for dogs.

Even in the cold of winter, the opportunity to be outdoors is a sensory adventure . . . Sniffing its surroundings is the equivalent of reading a newspaper for a dog: a log of who's been where and done what.

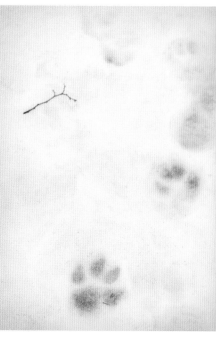

At that hour, the dogs of the Upper West Side were returning from their morning walks, streaming out of the park's Eighty-First Street entrance. It was quite a show. This is one of the dressier parts of the city, and about half the dogs were wearing rain slickers, their bright colors contrasting with the livery of the doormen they often stopped to greet.

JOHN HOMANS (Writer and editor)

Sculpture restoration made possible
through the generosity of
Sidney and Arthur Diamond
1988

MISCHKA

There weren't too many people out with their dogs on this cold and snowy morning in Central Park, but among the few were Mischka and Rocketman. While Andy and I were talking with Caroline, the dogs' owner, Rocketman (overleaf) lay still on the cold, icy pavement, head down, patiently waiting for his ball game to recommence. Meanwhile, Mischka stood at the edge of the fountain, obviously looking for something. When I asked what it was she was looking for, Caroline explained that a while ago, Mischka had found a raccoon nesting on the centerpiece of the fountain, and had been waiting for it to return ever since.

FRANKLIN

On our way home from a playground one evening, Charlize and I had the pleasure of meeting Franklin, the most adorable French bulldog puppy, as wide as he is long. I just had to photograph this little guy; he was too cute! After explaining about the project and exchanging contact details, I managed to drag Charlize away, eager to get home to check my diary to arrange a time to photograph Franklin before he got too much bigger!

Summer in the Big Apple is hot. But steamy sidewalks can be replaced by beaches for dogs to run free and feel the wind whipping through their fur and the sand beneath their paws.

ARAGON (K-9 2007)

"I purchased him to be a police dog when he was eight months old. Normally we wait until they're a year old before we begin training them, but he was a very good candidate. Two out of four dogs are successful in the initial training program. Then, to join the Urban Search and Rescue program for FEMA (Federal Emergency Management Agency), they train for 1,200 hours. Basically we're looking for dogs that have a 'built-in light switch.' Aragon is very clear in his job. He could be out looking for a bad guy and a building could collapse in Manhattan and he'd immediately start searching for a live victim under the collapsed structure. After the earthquake in Haiti in 2010, we were sending rescue dogs into places that were way too dangerous for people—that's why we were sending them in there. Believe it or not, they're so willing to do it. It can be scary at times, but it's their job and they love it. Aragon and I received a New York State Liberty Award from New York Senator Charles J. Fuschillo, Jr. for our search and rescue efforts in Haiti.

Aragon lives at home with me and my wife and kids, and two teacup Chihuahuas. The four-pound female Chihuahua is top dog at home. She tries to stop him from going to work by holding on to his tail. It's really funny. He's a very social animal. When we come home at night he'll go and check on the kids and do his rounds. It's typical of his breed because he's a herding dog, so he'll make sure everybody's in the house. I really was very, very lucky to get that dog. He's a super dog. I just have so much faith in him."

Police Officer Scott Mateyaschuk
New York Police Department

"It's not all about puppy love.
Adopt an older dog,
and you'll get loved back
more than you ever imagined."

Humane Society of New York

THE HUMANE SOCIETY OF NEW YORK

Since 1904, the Humane Society of New York (HSNY) has been a continual presence in New York City, caring for animals in need when illness, injury, or homelessness strikes. Originally founded to protect the city's working horses from abuse, services have since expanded, and currently the HSNY veterinary clinic and adoption center care for more than 38,000 animals each year. HSNY provides comprehensive, affordable medical care, seven days a week, and is responsible for hundreds of animals with diverse needs. Some of the many programs offered include Humane Education and the Animal Mukti Free Spay/Neuter Program, and for those people with financial difficulties, the Society underwrites the cost of life-saving veterinary care through their Animal Emergency Appeal. For these people, the Society may be the only place to turn to for medical help for their animals.

HSNY's Vladimir Horowitz & Wanda Toscanini Horowitz Adoption Center is a unique shelter where homeless animals live and thrive until they are placed in loving, responsible homes. In addition to any medical care that they might need, all adoption animals are spayed or neutered, vaccinated, and microchipped. Along with providing physical necessities, the Society also meets the animals' emotional needs. All of the dogs for adoption are evaluated and put on training programs by the Director of Animal Behavior, Broadway's Tony Award–winning champion of the shelter dog, Bill Berloni (see page 106).

Dogs have always been a part of my life. When I was a small child, my first companion dog was a brown lion Pekingese named Bonnie Nuts, and I loved him dearly. He went with me wherever he was allowed to go, occasionally chewing up a few of my dolls along the way!

His was a very reassuring presence for me. Sleeping by my bed at night, he was my friend and I always felt his devotion. He was with me for as many years as he could be until age and time took him from me. He left me with memories that started me on a lifetime of joyful relationships with countless other dogs, and for this, I will always be grateful.

If there is one thing I know, it is that dogs bring love, companionship, humor, joy, and protection to our lives and, I believe, they deserve the same measure of care and protection to be brought to their lives in return.

Virginia Chipurnoi, President
The Humane Society of New York

ACKNOWLEDGMENTS

To finally get to create a collection of images in one of my favorite cities of the world has been an incredible experience. Working on *The New York Dog* has been one of the most personally rewarding projects I have completed to date. I have met so many amazing people who have assisted and supported us during our time in New York, and every dog and owner that I have met and worked with has been so incredibly enthusiastic and encouraging; thank you all.

My husband, Andrew, how do I thank you? This project has been as much yours as it has been mine. You have put your heart and soul into this, and I could not have done it without you. "Thank you" just does not seem enough to say, you truly have been amazing! Along with arranging shoots, writing up proposals, finding locations, and assisting me when needed, you also created some brilliant video footage of the project; to have this alongside the images I have created makes our memories all the more special and real. To the full "Team McKenna": what an experience! Andy, our daughter, Charlize, and our live-in friend and Charlize-minder, Hannah Cox: You all have been troopers. Being in New York and working on this project has been a true team effort, and given us many memories I know we will treasure forever. Thank you from the bottom of my heart for your support, encouragement, and understanding of my long hours and daily shoots.

A million and one thanks go to all the dogs and their owners, especially Darcy and Ollie, who have been such a support to both Andy and me, and given us so much hope for our future, which we hope will take us back to New York soon. James and Ginetta, with Valentino and Geisha, you have become such wonderful friends; your assistance and kindness along with your friendship have made our time in New York even more special. Priscilla and Piper, you welcomed us into your home and treated us as part of your family—thank you so much for the time we spent with you and the memories we will never forget. Rest assured, we will be back! Ryan Lee and Clio, it has been great to get to know you. Thank you so much for your support and assistance during the project; yours is yet another friendship that will be continued. A huge thanks to Tom Hickey and Merlin; our chance meeting one morning not only led to me creating some gorgeous images for the book, but also enabled us to build a great friendship and business relationship. Thank you so much for all the wonderful design skills you have contributed to the development of our website. Richard and Popcorn, thank you so much for all your assistance with bringing together the location for your portrait. And finally, Lenny. You know who you are! I know you don't want or need any publicity, but we are so grateful for your time and generosity.

A book would never come to fruition if it did not have the support of a publisher. In the case of *The New York Dog*, I have had the honor of having the support of both my long-standing publisher, PQ Blackwell, along with the on-hand support and assistance from my New York–based publishers, Abrams. Thank you to everyone involved—you have no idea how much I really do appreciate your support. A huge thank you especially to those at Abrams who gave me the opportunity to work with two of my all-time favorite photographers, Albert Watson and William Wegman; to have the chance to meet and photograph them with their dogs was a dream come true. Also, a special mention to Leslie Stoker and her dog Riley, pictured left.

To the team at the Humane Society of New York (HSNY): having witnessed firsthand the amazing work you do has confirmed my decision to support this wonderful organization with proceeds from the sales of this book; you truly are a remarkable animal shelter. A huge thank you to Sandra DeFeo: You live and breathe the HSNY, and Andy and I are incredibly grateful for the time you allocated to us to assist us throughout this project.

A huge thank you to Hasselblad UK for supplying me with an H4 system to create the images for *The New York Dog* project. I have been a supporter and user of Hasselblad ever since I first started capturing images in my late teens, so to have the opportunity to work with this magnificent piece of machinery was wonderful.

To our dear friends Andrew and Bec Harrison from New Zealand, your support and assistance to us during our time in New York has been so unbelievably kind; thank you from the bottom of our hearts.

Jo Grams and Johannes Van Kan, thank you both for being so generous with your time and for assisting us with our business development—you are wonderful friends, and your belief in us gives us so much more strength.

Tracy and Franz, thank you so much for all your assistance and for our newfound friendship—you both have made our New York experience such a life-changing one. The use of your apartment has led us to meet so many wonderful new friends—when we move back, let's hope we can join your "Melrose Place" community.

Alice Merino, thank you so much for all the time and assistance you gave us, gathering together such wonderful dogs to photograph on Staten Island. You have been so great to work with and are yet another person who has left a lasting impression in our lives.

Julio Rivera, you have been such a wonderful help with arranging dogs in Queens for me to photograph. The stories you shared with me about the dogs and owners you have assisted in difficult situations only strengthens my view of how much you care for the dogs you work with. Thank you so much for donating your time and your talents.

A huge thank you to the New York Palace for allowing me to photograph in your stunning hotel, and a special thank you to Lauren Rebholz for being so fantastic and making our time working at the Palace so enjoyable. We are looking forward to working with you further in the future.

Thank you so much to Robine Harris for your assistance with the post-production on some of the images for the book. You stepped in at the last minute to help me make my deadline, and though under pressure, you managed to use your magic touch and enhance my images with the perfect amount of subtlety to make them shine. It is great to have you back on the team. Thank you!

To the people who donated to our Indiegogo campaign to help fund the creation of images for *The New York Dog* book, thank you so much—this project would not have eventuated without your support. Thank you especially to Andrew and Rebecca Harrison and Carolyn Nesgos for your generous donations.

To all the dogs I didn't get to photograph: New York is a city with thousands of dogs. There is only one of me, only a smidgeon of time, and only a certain number of pages in the book. I feel terrible that not everyone that approached me had the opportunity to get their dog photographed—believe me, I would have photographed them all if I could have. I will be back in New York, though, so your chance to have your precious pup photographed by me is not out of reach.

Last but not least, to my and Andy's families: Thank you for your continuous support and encouragement. It is a shame that you only got to share in this fantastic adventure via Skype, but we hope you will visit us in New York once we set foot back there in the near future. We will have more time ourselves then to join you on your Big Apple adventure.

New York, you are an inspiring city—thank you for such an incredible six months!

Rachael Hale McKenna

IMAGE CREDITS

Front cover and page 16: Bango (Goldendoodle), SoHo, Manhattan; back cover: Clio (Border terrier) and Jordin (Jack Russell terrier), Red Hook, Brooklyn; case and p. 51: Olive (boxer), 5Pointz, Long Island City, Queens; front endpaper: First row, left to right: Manhattan Bridge, DUMBO, Brooklyn; hot chocolate, Chelsea, Manhattan; Cubby (crossbreed), Midtown, Manhattan; Downtown, Manhattan; Central Park; Union Square, Manhattan. Second row, left to right: Mirror detail, Felix Restaurant, SoHo, Manhattan; Union Square, Manhattan; Central Park; under the Williamsburg Bridge; TriBeCa, Manhattan; Daysee (crossbreed), the New York Dog Nanny (dog daycare), Manhattan. Third row, left to right: Gramercy Park, Manhattan; Charlize and Rachael meeting Lucy (French bulldog), Chelsea, Manhattan; rainy day reflection, West Village, Manhattan; Riley (beabull), Greenwich Village, Manhattan; Fifth Avenue, Manhattan; New York subway. Fourth row, left to right: Geisha (Pekingese), Washington Heights, Manhattan; Shelby (German shepherd cross), Central Park; stacked chairs, Metropolitan Building, Queens; Rachael, Charlize, and Ginetta with Valentino (German shepherd cross), Washington Heights, Manhattan; sewing machines, All Saints store display, SoHo, Manhattan; view of Manhattan from the Manhattan Bridge.

Pages 2–3: Rebecca and Gabriel (Yorkshire terrier), Fifth Avenue, Manhattan; p. 4: Tiki (English bull terrier), Jersey Street, SoHo, Manhattan; p. 6: Georgina Bloomberg with her five rescue dogs, Mabel, Mona, Hugo, Stella, and Chopper, and her rescue pig Wilbur, North Salem, New York; p. 8: Atticus (great Dane), Red Hook, Brooklyn; p. 10: Poets' Walk, Central Park; p. 11: Sobhre (Afghan hound) and Piper (standard poodle), Central Park; p. 12: Dog walker Kevin crossing Central Park West; p. 13: Terrence with Skyla (American pit bull) and T-T (Pomeranian), Harlem; pp. 14–15: Frankie (Labrador cross), DUMBO, Brooklyn; p. 17: Clockwise, top left: Frankie and Bodega (Shiba Inu), Chelsea, Manhattan; mosaic detail, East Village, Manhattan; Captain (Maltipoo), TriBeCa, Manhattan; coffee break, SoHo, Manhattan; Felix restaurant, SoHo, Manhattan; p. 18: Katrina and Twiga (greyhound), Greene Street, SoHo, Manhattan; p. 20: Pork Chop (French bulldog/Boston cross), DUMBO, Brooklyn; p. 21: Eddie and Axel (dogue de Bordeaux), courthouse steps, Downtown, Manhattan; pp. 22–23: Berton and Atticus (great Dane), Red Hook, Brooklyn; p. 24: Riley (beabull), Greenwich Village, Manhattan; p. 26: Clockwise, top left: Light store, East Village, Manhattan; Daisy (Maltese cross), Midtown, Manhattan; Via and Buddy (Yorkshire terrier), East Village subway station, Manhattan; p. 27: Floyd (Goldendoodle), Mr. Joseph's barber shop, West Village, Manhattan; pp. 28–29: Via and Buddy (Yorkshire terrier), on the L Train, Manhattan; p. 31: Roxy (possible boxer/Dalmatian cross), Fort Greene, Brooklyn; pp. 32–33: Max (standard poodle), Elizabeth Street, Nolita, Manhattan; p. 34: Café detail, TriBeCa, Manhattan; p. 35: Larry (English cream-colored dachshund), Williamsburg, Brooklyn; pp. 36, 37: George (American bulldog), Williamsburg, Brooklyn; p. 38: Cam and Pork Chop (French bulldog/Boston cross), DUMBO, Brooklyn; p. 40: Clockwise, top left: Lizzie (Welsh springer spaniel), East Village, Manhattan; building detail, Chelsea, Manhattan; Z (harlequin great Dane), Carroll Gardens, Brooklyn; Zoe (crossbreed), Amber (pit bull cross), and Mr. Belvedere Jones (Shih Tzu), Queens; street signs, DUMBO, Brooklyn; p. 41: Z (harlequin great Dane), Brooklyn Farmacy & Soda Fountain, Carroll Gardens, Brooklyn; p. 42: Boston terriers, Central Park; p. 44: Atticus (great Dane), Red Hook, Brooklyn; p. 45: Z (harlequin great Dane), Carroll Gardens, Brooklyn; p. 46: Carolyn and Sammy (Chihuahua), Fifth Avenue, Manhattan; p. 47: Clockwise, top left: Building detail, DUMBO, Brooklyn; Bullet (American pit bull), 5Pointz, Long Island City, Queens; Atticus (great Dane), Red Hook, Brooklyn; p. 48: Manhattan Bridge, DUMBO, Brooklyn; p. 49: Reno (Alaskan Malamute), Meatpacking District, Manhattan; p. 50: Tiki (English bull terrier), SoHo, Manhattan; p. 52: Miki (wire-haired fox terrier), TriBeCa, Manhattan; p. 53: Albert Watson and Miki (wire-haired fox terrier), TriBeCa, Manhattan; pp. 54–55: Albert Watson and Miki (wire-haired fox terrier), TriBeCa, Manhattan; p. 56: Lily and Reykjavik (harlequin great Danes), DUMBO, Brooklyn; p. 58: Gemma (pit bull cross) and Bullet (American pit bull), 5Pointz, Long Island City, Queens; p. 59: Lily (English bulldog), Williamsburg, Brooklyn; pp. 60–61: View of Brooklyn from the Manhattan Bridge; p. 62: Amber (pit bull

cross), Queens; p. 63: Amber (pit bull cross), Kush (American Staffordshire terrier), Mr. Belvedere Jones (Shih Tzu), and Zoe (crossbreed), Queens; p. 64: Bru (Australian shepherd), Central Park; p. 65: Clockwise, top left: Dog walker April with her clients' dogs, Central Park; Upper East Side boardwalk, Manhattan; Gia (Yorkshire terrier), Chelsea, Manhattan; Bryant Park, Manhattan; mosaic detail, East Village, Manhattan; pp. 66–67: Pixel (Lakeland terrier), Central Park; p. 68: Zoe (Yorkiepoo), Central Park; p. 70: Angus (West Highland terrier), Central Park; p. 71: Drummer (Labrador retriever), Prospect Park, Brooklyn; p. 72: Charlize with Gravy (crossbreed), Fort Greene Park, Brooklyn; p. 74: Bear (soft-coated wheaten terrier) and Bella (golden retriever), Central Park; p. 75: Sammy (foxhound), Prospect Park, Brooklyn; pp. 76–77: Jazz (Newfoundland cross) and Morgan (golden retriever), Prospect Park, Brooklyn; p. 78: Roxy (possible boxer/Dalmatian cross), Fort Greene Park, Brooklyn; p. 80: Clockwise, top left: Theodore Roosevelt Park, Upper West Side, Manhattan; Laurent and Zoe (Yorkiepoo), Upper East Side, Manhattan; Aries (crossbreed), Prospect Park, Brooklyn; Brooklyn Heights, Brooklyn; Zoe (Yorkiepoo), Central Park; p. 81: Rocco (basenji cross), Central Park; p. 82: Sammy (foxhound), Prospect Park, Brooklyn; p. 84: Pluto (terrier cross), Fort Greene, Brooklyn; p. 85: Tracy Middendorf and Pluto (terrier cross), Fort Greene, Brooklyn; p. 86: Cornelia Winston Whitney Hay and Webster Westbrook Alexander Hay (Cavalier King Charles spaniels), Upper West Side, Manhattan; p. 87: Clockwise, top left: Morgan (golden retriever), Jazz (Newfoundland cross), and a Boston terrier, Prospect Park, Brooklyn; Suki (terrier cross), Prospect Park, Brooklyn; Gravy and Biscuit (crossbreeds), Fort Greene Park, Brooklyn; Griff (Brussels griffon), Central Park; Sheep Meadow, Central Park; p. 88: Dog walker Christian with his clients' dogs, Brooklyn Heights, Brooklyn; p. 90: West Village, Manhattan; pp. 91, 92: Topper (Weimaraner), Chelsea, Manhattan; p. 93: William Wegman with Flo, Topper, Candy, and Bobbin (Weimaraners), Chelsea, Manhattan; p. 94: Clockwise, top left: Building detail, Union Square, Manhattan; Nicky (schnauzer), Water Mill, Long Island; Cheryl and Lily (English bulldog), Williamsburg, Brooklyn; Gravy (crossbreed), Fort Greene, Brooklyn; mirror hall, Metropolitan Building, Queens; p. 95: Cubby (crossbreed), Midtown, Manhattan; pp. 96–97: Webster Westbrook Alexander Hay and Cornelia Winston Whitney Hay (Cavalier King Charles spaniels), Upper West Side, Manhattan; p. 99: Ollie (Labradoodle), Midtown, Manhattan; p. 100: Maddy (miniature Australian shepherd), The Drawing Room, New York Palace Hotel, Midtown, Manhattan; p. 101: Louis opens the door for Hannah, Mousse (Havanese), and Doolin (Shih Tzu), New York Palace Hotel, Midtown, Manhattan; p. 102: Charlie (Yorkshire terrier), The Library, New York Palace Hotel, Midtown, Manhattan; p. 103: Mary and Charlie (Yorkshire terrier), The Villard Mansion, New York Palace Hotel, Midtown, Manhattan; p. 104: Valentino (German shepherd cross) and Geisha (Pekingese), Washington Heights, Manhattan; p. 106: Bill Berloni with Sunny (crossbreed), the lead dog in the Annie Broadway production, Broadway Theatre, Manhattan; p. 107: Sunny (crossbreed) in her dressing room, Broadway Theatre, Manhattan; p. 108: Ollie (Labradoodle), Manhattan; p. 109: Miki (wire-haired fox terrier), TriBeCa, Manhattan; p. 110: Mona (Cane Corso), Alice Austin House, Staten Island; p. 111: Snowy (miniature poodle), Queens; p. 112: London (Weimaraner), Staten Island; p. 113: Clockwise, top left: Harry and Alice (terrier crosses), Brooklyn; Bethesda Fountain, Central Park; Pluto (Cockerpoo), Staten Island; Winnie and Moses (golden retrievers), Central Park; Winston (corgi), Fort Greene, Brooklyn; p. 114: Sebastian and Gabriella with Floyd (Goldendoodle), West Village, Manhattan; p. 115: Tanesha and Jordin (Jack Russell terrier), Red Hook, Brooklyn; p. 116: Bernard (Yorkshire terrier), Williamsburg, Brooklyn; p. 117: Chinatown, Manhattan; p. 118: Oscar (pit bull cross), Queens; p. 120: Sophia and Feng with Tilly (border collie cross), Children's Magical Garden, East Village, Manhattan; p. 121: Richard and Popcorn (Weimaraner), Chinatown, Manhattan; pp. 122–23: Olive (boxer) and Moxie (pit bull cross), 5Pointz, Long Island City, Queens; p. 124: Zac with Redmond (Saint Bernard) and Monty (crossbreed), Book Court Bookstore, Cobble Hill, Brooklyn; p. 126: Emma (crossbreed), Williamsburg, Brooklyn; p. 127: Winston (corgi), Fort Greene, Brooklyn; p. 128: Katrina and Twiga (greyhound), SoHo, Manhattan; p. 129: Clockwise, top left: American flag, Chinatown, Manhattan; Larry (English cream-colored dachshund), Williamsburg, Brooklyn; Gemma (pit bull cross), Queens; Twiga (greyhound), SoHo, Manhattan; George (American bulldog), Williamsburg, Brooklyn; p. 130: Clio (Border terrier) and Jordin (Jack Russell terrier), Red Hook, Brooklyn; p. 132: Merlin (pit bull cross), DUMBO, Brooklyn; pp. 134–35: Celeste (terrier cross) and Ollie (Labradoodle), Bethesda Fountain, Central Park; pp. 136, 137: Valentino (German shepherd cross), Fort Tryon Park, Manhattan; p. 138: Dog walker, Poets' Walk, Central Park; p. 139: Ruby (crossbreed), Central Park; p. 140: Clockwise, top left: Tela (bullmastiff), Central Park; Bryant Park, Manhattan; Valentino (German shepherd cross), Fort Tryon Park, Manhattan; Paw prints in the snow, Central Park; Guinness and Lucky (crossbreeds), Central Park; p. 141: Mateo (dogue de Bordeaux), Central Park; p. 142: Geisha (Pekingese), Fort Tryon Park, Manhattan; p. 144: Mischka (Japanese Akita), Bethesda Fountain, Central Park; pp. 146–47: Rocketman (crossbreed), Central Park; p. 148: pit bull cross and Hungarian vizla, Central Park; p. 149: Jessi and Lara (Hungarian vizlas), Central Park; p. 150: Franklin (French bulldog), Stuyvesant Town, Manhattan; pp. 152–53: Charlize and Piper (standard poodle), Cutchogue, Long Island; p. 154: Kobe (Irish wolfhound), Staten Island; p. 155: Clockwise, top left: Amy with Geisha (Bernese mountain dog) and Panda (Landseer Newfoundland), Amagansett Beach, Long Island; Nicky (schnauzer), Bridgehampton, Long Island; Panda (Landseer Newfoundland), Amagansett Beach, Long Island; p. 156: Scott and Aragon (German shepherd), New York Police Department training facility, Brooklyn; pp. 158–59: Jinx (crossbreed), Jake (terrier cross), and Brody (soft-coated wheaten terrier), Staten Island; p. 160: Willis (Chinese hairless crested cross), the mascot of the Humane Society of New York, Midtown East, Manhattan; p. 162: Various images captured at the Humane Society of New York's premises, Midtown East, Manhattan; p. 164: Riley (beabull), Greenwich Village, Manhattan; p. 168: Moxie (pit bull cross), 5Pointz, Long Island City, Queens.

Back endpaper: First row, left to right: Williamsburg shoreline, Brooklyn; West Eighteenth Street, Manhattan; sign, TriBeCa, Manhattan; Rachael photographing Eddie and Axel (dogue de Bordeaux), courthouse steps, Downtown, Manhattan; looking back to Manhattan; building, TriBeCa, Manhattan. Second row, left to right: Dog walking in a rainstorm, West Village, Manhattan; Country Store, Long Island; sign, Williamsburg, Brooklyn; sunset, Chelsea, Manhattan; East Village building, Manhattan; Valentino, Fort Tryon Park, Manhattan. Third row, left to right: Felix Restaurant, SoHo, Manhattan; Dougal (poodle), Central Park; DUMBO, Brooklyn; Manhattan public space; Charlize on Jane's Carousel, DUMBO, Brooklyn; George (American bulldog), Fort Greene, Brooklyn. Bottom row, left to right: Rachael photographing Pork Chop (French bulldog/Boston terrier cross), Brooklyn; street party, West Village, Manhattan; Charlize and Hannah, Cutchogue; Axel (dogue de Bordeaux), Downtown, Manhattan; view from the Highline, Chelsea, Manhattan; Charlize, Gramercy Park, Manhattan.

The making of this book would not have been possible without the generous support of Hasselblad, The New York Palace, and The Humane Society of New York.

HASSELBLAD

www.hasselbladusa.com

THE
NEW YORK PALACE

www.newyorkpalace.com

www.humanesocietyny.org

Library of Congress Control Number: 2013945650

ISBN: 978-1-61769-090-7

Produced and originated by PQ Blackwell Limited
116 Symonds Street, Auckland 1010, New Zealand
www.pqblackwell.com

Text: Rachael Hale McKenna
Book design: Helene Dehmer
Editorial: Jo Garden and Rachel Clare

Printed and bound in China
10 9 8 7 6 5 4 3 2 1

Stewart, Tabori & Chang books are available at special discounts when purchased in quantity for premiums and promotions as well as fundraising or educational use. Special editions can also be created to specification. For details, contact specialsales@abramsbooks.com or the address below.

ABRAMS
THE ART OF BOOKS SINCE 1949
115 West 18th Street
New York, NY 10011
www.abramsbooks.com